SUPERPOWER SCIENCE

THE SUPERHUMAN BODY

JOY LIN

ILLUSTRATED BY ALAN BROWN

B.E.S.
PUBLISHING

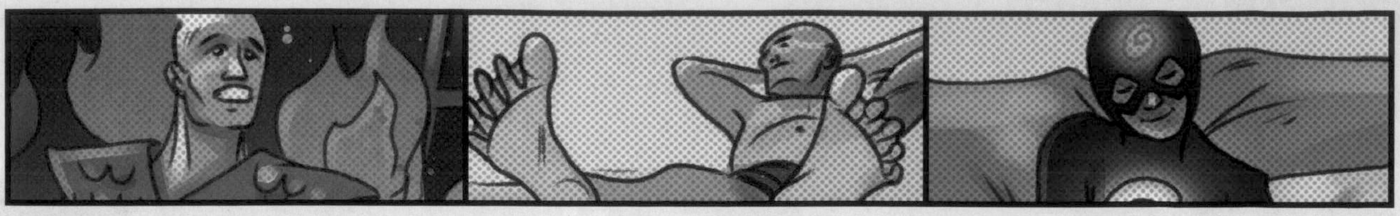

FIRST EDITION FOR THE UNITED STATES, ITS TERRITORIES AND DEPENDENCIES, THE PHILIPPINE REPUBLIC, AND CANADA PUBLISHED IN 2019 BY B.E.S. PUBLISHING CO.

FIRST PUBLISHED IN GREAT BRITAIN IN 2018 BY WAYLAND, AN IMPRINT OF HACHETTE CHILDREN'S GROUP, PART OF HODDER & STOUGHTON.

ALL INQUIRIES SHOULD BE ADDRESSED TO:
B.E.S. PUBLISHING CO.
250 WIRELESS BOULEVARD
HAUPPAUGE, NY 11788
WWW.BES-PUBLISHING.COM

ISBN: 978-1-4380-1268-1

LIBRARY OF CONGRESS CONTROL NUMBER: 2018951835

DATE OF MANUFACTURE: JANUARY 2019
MANUFACTURED BY: WKT, SHENZHEN, CHINA

PRINTED IN CHINA
9 8 7 6 5 4 3 2 1

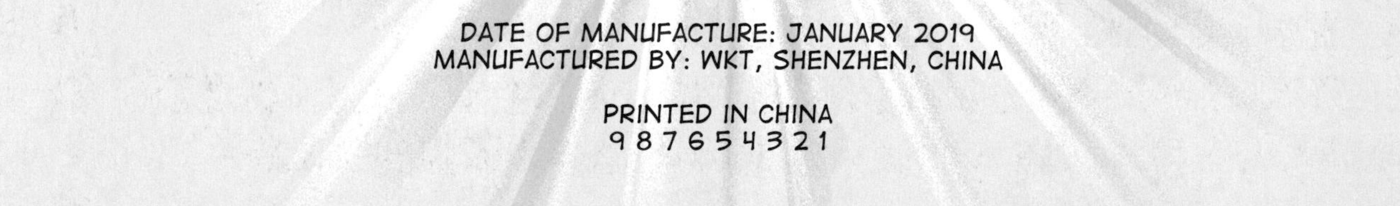

What if I had a superpower?

HAVEN'T WE ALL ASKED OURSELVES THIS QUESTION AT SOME POINT? IT WOULD BE AMAZING TO BE ABLE TO READ PEOPLE'S MINDS, REGENERATE ANY PART OF YOUR BODY, OR BE IMMORTAL. ARE THESE ABILITIES THE STUFF OF DREAMS OR WILL WE ONE DAY BE ABLE TO BE REAL-LIFE SUPERHEROES?

ONCE UPON A TIME WE WERE ONLY ABLE TO OBSERVE THE STARS FROM EARTH AND DREAM OF EXPLORING SPACE, THEN ONE DAY, WE SENT MEN TO THE MOON! SCIENCE IS DEFINITELY CATCHING UP WITH OUR IMAGINATIONS. LET'S SEE WHAT HAPPENS WHEN YOU APPLY THE LAWS OF SCIENCE TO SUPERPOWERS...

CONTENTS

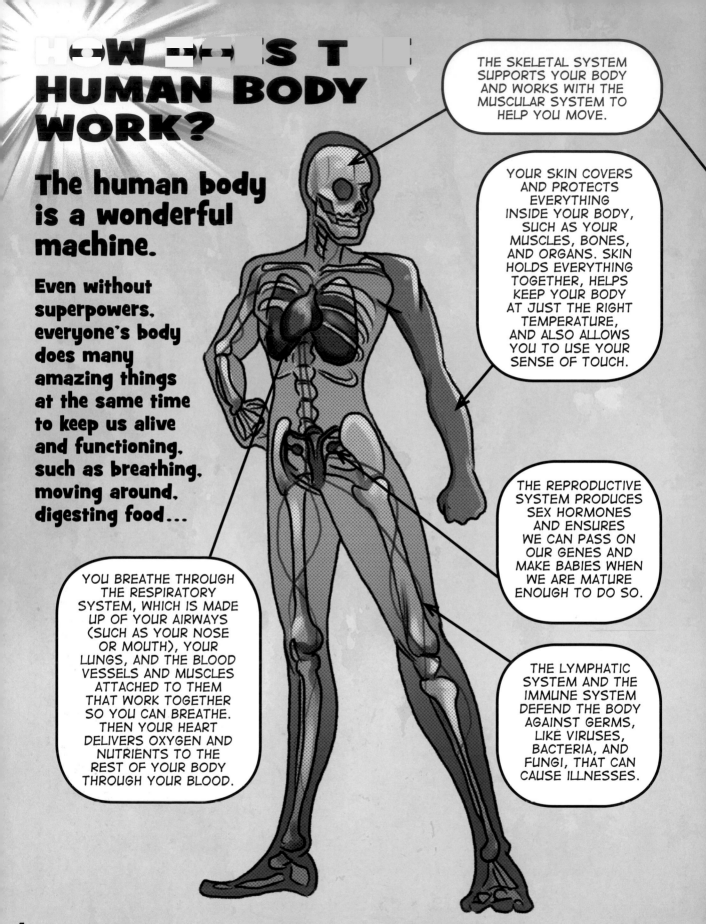

HOW DOES THE HUMAN BODY WORK?

The human body is a wonderful machine.

Even without superpowers, everyone's body does many amazing things at the same time to keep us alive and functioning, such as breathing, moving around, digesting food…

THE SKELETAL SYSTEM SUPPORTS YOUR BODY AND WORKS WITH THE MUSCULAR SYSTEM TO HELP YOU MOVE.

YOUR SKIN COVERS AND PROTECTS EVERYTHING INSIDE YOUR BODY, SUCH AS YOUR MUSCLES, BONES, AND ORGANS. SKIN HOLDS EVERYTHING TOGETHER, HELPS KEEP YOUR BODY AT JUST THE RIGHT TEMPERATURE, AND ALSO ALLOWS YOU TO USE YOUR SENSE OF TOUCH.

THE REPRODUCTIVE SYSTEM PRODUCES SEX HORMONES AND ENSURES WE CAN PASS ON OUR GENES AND MAKE BABIES WHEN WE ARE MATURE ENOUGH TO DO SO.

YOU BREATHE THROUGH THE RESPIRATORY SYSTEM, WHICH IS MADE UP OF YOUR AIRWAYS (SUCH AS YOUR NOSE OR MOUTH), YOUR LUNGS, AND THE BLOOD VESSELS AND MUSCLES ATTACHED TO THEM THAT WORK TOGETHER SO YOU CAN BREATHE. THEN YOUR HEART DELIVERS OXYGEN AND NUTRIENTS TO THE REST OF YOUR BODY THROUGH YOUR BLOOD.

THE LYMPHATIC SYSTEM AND THE IMMUNE SYSTEM DEFEND THE BODY AGAINST GERMS, LIKE VIRUSES, BACTERIA, AND FUNGI, THAT CAN CAUSE ILLNESSES.

THE NERVOUS SYSTEM, MADE UP OF YOUR BRAIN, SPINAL CORD, AND NERVES, ALLOWS COMMUNICATION BETWEEN DIFFERENT PARTS OF YOUR BODY, AND PROCESSES INFORMATION FROM THE OUTSIDE WORLD BY SENDING IT TO THE BRAIN, THE DECISION-MAKER.

THE ENDOCRINE SYSTEM PRODUCES HORMONES, WHICH ARE THE BODY'S CHEMICAL MESSENGERS, TRANSFERRING INFORMATION AND INSTRUCTIONS FROM ONE SET OF CELLS TO ANOTHER. THEY ALSO REGULATE BODILY PROCESSES.

THE DIGESTIVE SYSTEM, WHICH INCLUDES YOUR STOMACH, LIVER, AND INTESTINES, PROCESSES THE FOOD YOU EAT FOR ENERGY; THE URINARY SYSTEM, MADE UP OF YOUR KIDNEYS AND BLADDER, REMOVES WASTE.

YOU MIGHT BE SURPRISED TO LEARN THIS, BUT SOME SUPERHUMANS ALREADY EXIST! FINNISH OLYMPIC SKIING CHAMPION EERO MÄNTYRANTA (1937–2013) HAD A CONDITION CALLED PRIMARY FAMILIAL AND CONGENITAL POLYCYTHEMIA DUE TO A GENE MUTATION. BECAUSE OF IT, HE HAD THE ABILITY TO CARRY UP TO 50 PERCENT MORE OXYGEN IN HIS BLOOD, WHICH INCREASED HIS STAMINA AND MADE HIM A GREAT ATHLETE.

UNFORTUNATELY, GENETIC MUTATIONS DO NOT ALWAYS RESULT IN SUPERHUMANS AND CAN BE THE CAUSE OF ILLNESS AND DISABILITY. EVEN IF YOU WERE TO GAIN SUPERPOWERS, THERE ARE ALWAYS SOME UNFORESEEN CONSEQUENCES. LET'S SEE WHAT THEY ARE...

THE IRON WAVE:
SUPER SOLID TO SUPER LIQUID!

Wouldn't it be cool to suddenly turn into metal to protect yourself? Especially when a large object is about to fall on you!

OR TURN INTO WATER TO SQUEEZE THROUGH A TIGHT SPACE?

BUT, WAIT, HOW WOULD THAT AFFECT YOUR BODY?

IRON WAVE'S SUPERPOWERS

- to change his body into iron
- to turn his body into water
- great for protecting others or penetrating secure locations

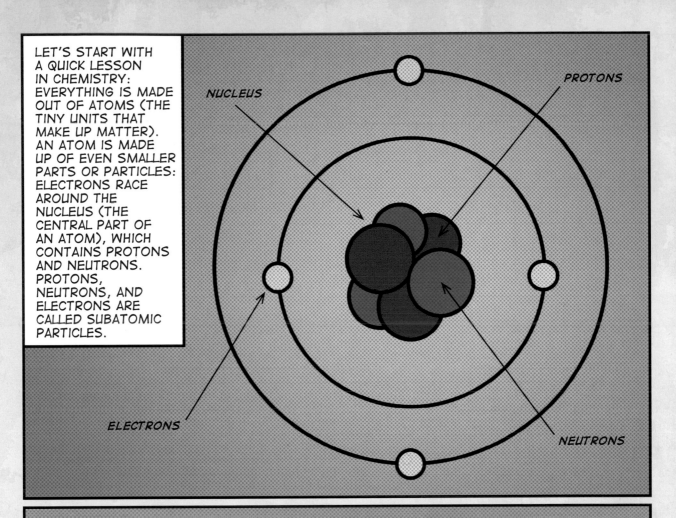

LET'S START WITH A QUICK LESSON IN CHEMISTRY: EVERYTHING IS MADE OUT OF ATOMS (THE TINY UNITS THAT MAKE UP MATTER). AN ATOM IS MADE UP OF EVEN SMALLER PARTS OR PARTICLES: ELECTRONS RACE AROUND THE NUCLEUS (THE CENTRAL PART OF AN ATOM), WHICH CONTAINS PROTONS AND NEUTRONS. PROTONS, NEUTRONS, AND ELECTRONS ARE CALLED SUBATOMIC PARTICLES.

NUCLEUS

PROTONS

ELECTRONS

NEUTRONS

MATTER MADE UP OF JUST ONE TYPE OF ATOM IS CALLED AN ELEMENT. EVERY ELEMENT HAS ITS OWN SPECIFIC NUMBER OF PROTONS, AND WE CALL THIS ITS ATOMIC NUMBER. IT IS HOW WE DEFINE AN ELEMENT AND ALSO HOW THE PERIODIC TABLE, WHICH SETS OUT THE ELEMENTS, IS ORDERED.

THE PERIODIC TABLE

NOW, LET'S EXPLORE WHAT ELEMENTS A HUMAN BODY IS MADE OUT OF. A TYPICAL HUMAN BODY CONTAINS ROUGHLY 65 PERCENT OXYGEN, 18 PERCENT CARBON, 10 PERCENT HYDROGEN, AND 7 PERCENT OF A FEW OTHER ELEMENTS.

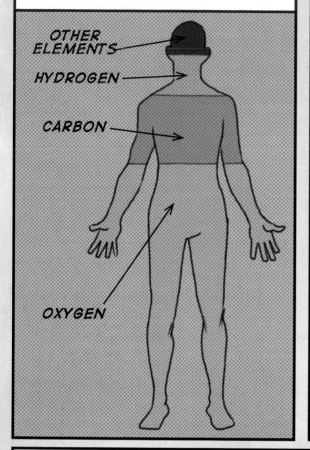

OTHER ELEMENTS

HYDROGEN

CARBON

OXYGEN

SO, IF YOU WERE GOING TO USE YOUR SUPERPOWER AND TURN YOUR BODY INTO IRON, WHERE WOULD THE IRON COME FROM? WHAT SETS IRON (KNOWN AS Fe IN THE PERIODIC TABLE) APART FROM OTHER ELEMENTS IS THE FACT THAT IT HAS 26 PROTONS IN ITS NUCLEUS. IN IRON'S MOST COMMON FORM, IT HAS 30 NEUTRONS.

IRON

OXYGEN HAS EIGHT PROTONS AND EIGHT NEUTRONS, CARBON HAS SIX OF EACH, AND HYDROGEN ONLY HAS ONE PROTON. WE WOULD NEED TO ADD UP AND RESHUFFLE A LOT OF THESE ATOMS TO HAVE ENOUGH PROTONS AND NEUTRONS TO MAKE JUST ONE IRON ATOM.

THIS COMBINING PROCESS IS CALLED NUCLEAR FUSION, AND IT REQUIRES TREMENDOUS AMOUNTS OF HEAT AND PRESSURE TO HAPPEN, SO MUCH SO THAT THE ONLY NATURAL OCCURRENCE OF IT IS IN THE CENTER OF STARS.

EVEN IF YOUR BODY COULD SURVIVE THE HEAT, THE PEOPLE AND THE THINGS AROUND YOU WOULDN'T BECAUSE WHEN FUSION HAPPENS, IT PRODUCES A HUGE AMOUNT OF HEAT, TOO.

WHAT IF YOU WANTED TO USE YOUR OTHER SUPERPOWER AND TURN INTO WATER? A WATER MOLECULE, H_2O, IS MADE OUT OF 2 HYDROGEN ATOMS AND 1 OXYGEN ATOM AND AS WE'VE SEEN, A HUMAN BODY HAS PLENTY OF HYDROGEN AND OXYGEN!

BUT WHAT ABOUT ALL THE CARBON AND OTHER ELEMENTS? IN ORDER TO MAKE A WATER MOLECULE, WE COULD BREAK APART A BUNCH OF CARBON ATOMS AND REPACKAGE THE PROTONS TO BECOME WATER, RIGHT?

THIS DISASSEMBLY PROCESS IS CALLED NUCLEAR FISSION, AND ALSO REQUIRES TREMENDOUS ENERGY. ONCE THE CARBON ATOMS ARE BROKEN APART, THE LOOSE PROTONS AND NEUTRONS STILL REQUIRE FUSION TO CREATE OXYGEN, WHICH HAS 2 MORE PROTONS THAN CARBON DOES. AND WE ALL KNOW WHAT HAPPENS WHEN FUSION IS INVOLVED...A HUGE AMOUNT OF HEAT AND DESTRUCTION!

WHAT HAVE I DONE?

SO WHATEVER MATERIAL YOU TURN YOUR BODY INTO, IT INVOLVES NUCLEAR FUSION, WHICH IS HARMFUL TO YOU AND EVERYONE AROUND YOU.

ALSO, REMEMBER ALL THOSE BODY SYSTEMS WE LEARNED ABOUT IN THE INTRODUCTION (PP 4-5)? IF YOUR BODY WAS TURNED INTO METAL, HOW WOULD YOU MOVE AROUND WITHOUT A SKELETAL SYSTEM AND MUSCULAR SYSTEM? SINCE METAL DOESN'T STRETCH THE WAY NORMAL SKIN DOES, AND YOU ARE NOT MADE OUT OF SMALL PLATES THE WAY METAL ARMOR IS, YOU'D BE STUCK IN THE SAME PLACE FOREVER, LIKE A STATUE!

OR IF YOUR BODY WAS COMPLETELY TURNED INTO WATER, HOW WOULD YOU BE ABLE TO STAND UP WITHOUT A SKELETON TO SUPPORT YOU?

WORMS CAN MOVE FORWARD WITHOUT A SKELETON, BUT THAT'S BECAUSE THEY HAVE MUSCLES THAT STRETCH AND CONTRACT TO PUSH THEIR BODIES ALONG THE GROUND. HOW WOULD YOU TRAVEL AROUND WITHOUT ANY MUSCLES? WOULD A HELPFUL FRIEND CARRY YOU AROUND IN A BUCKET?

THANKS FOR CARRYING ME!

AND HOW WOULD YOU KEEP YOURSELF TOGETHER WITHOUT A LAYER OF SKIN TO PROTECT YOU FROM BEING ABSORBED BY THE CARPET BENEATH YOU?

EVEN IF YOU COULD MOVE, HOW WOULD YOU KNOW WHAT TO DO WITHOUT A BRAIN TO PROCESS INFORMATION AND A NERVOUS SYSTEM TO SEND SIGNALS TO THE REST OF YOU?

HOW WOULD YOU BREATHE WITHOUT THE RESPIRATORY SYSTEM? HOW WOULD YOUR BODY GET THE OXYGEN IT NEEDS WITHOUT THE CARDIOVASCULAR SYSTEM? THE ANSWER IS, NONE OF IT WOULD BE POSSIBLE...

WILL WE EVER BE ABLE TO TURN INTO METAL OR WATER? PROBABLY NOT. THOUGH SOME WOULD SAY THAT WE ARE ALREADY MOSTLY WATER: UP TO 65 PERCENT OF THE ADULT HUMAN BODY IS WATER! DO WE REALLY NEED THE LAST 35 PERCENT?

AS FOR TURNING INTO METAL, CONSIDER THE ADVANCES IN SCIENCE AND TECHNOLOGY FOR PROSTHETICS. PROSTHETICS ARE ARTIFICIAL LIMBS USED BY PEOPLE WHO HAVE LOST LIMBS THROUGH INJURY OR AMPUTATION. PROSTHETICS ENABLE PEOPLE TO WALK, RUN, CYCLE, AND HOLD OBJECTS. THEY CAN COME IN THE FORM OF ALMOST ANY BODY PART—INCLUDING ARMS, LEGS, AND HANDS—AND ARE MADE OF MATERIALS SUCH AS METAL, CARBON FIBER, OR PLASTIC.

SOME PEOPLE WITH PROSTHETIC LIMBS HAVEN'T LET THAT STOP THEM FROM BECOMING ATHLETES AND WINNING MEDALS. I THINK IT'S SAFE TO SAY THEY ALREADY HAVE SUPERHUMAN BODIES!

MIND-READING MAYA:
SHE CAN HEAR YOUR THOUGHTS!

Who wouldn't want to be able to hear people's thoughts?

 MIND-READING MAYA'S SUPERPOWERS
- to hear people's thoughts (known as telepathy)
- great for preventing disasters before they happen

YOU'D FIND OUT WHAT PEOPLE REALLY THINK ABOUT YOU.

I'M SO GLAD SHE'S MY FRIEND. SHE'S THE BEST!

AND EVEN FIND OUT WHAT A BAD GUY IS GOING TO DO BEFORE HE HAS ACTUALLY DONE IT!

I CAN RETIRE AFTER ROBBING THIS LAST BANK.

BUT IF YOU ARE TELEPATHIC, THEN YOU WOULD BE TELEPATHIC ALL THE TIME. IF YOU HAVE THE ABILITY TO RECEIVE THIS INFORMATION, YOU WOULD CONSTANTLY BE RECEIVING IT. THERE WOULD BE NO WAY TO TELL YOUR BRAIN TO TURN IT OFF.

I LOVE YOUR OUTFIT!

UGH, SO UGLY...

IMAGINE IF YOU WERE HAVING A CONVERSATION WITH SOMEONE WHO DOES NOT ALWAYS SAY WHAT THEY THINK. YOU'D BETTER WATCH THEIR MOUTH CAREFULLY SO YOU'D KNOW WHAT THEY ARE ACTUALLY SAYING OUT LOUD AS OPPOSED TO WHAT THEY ARE THINKING.

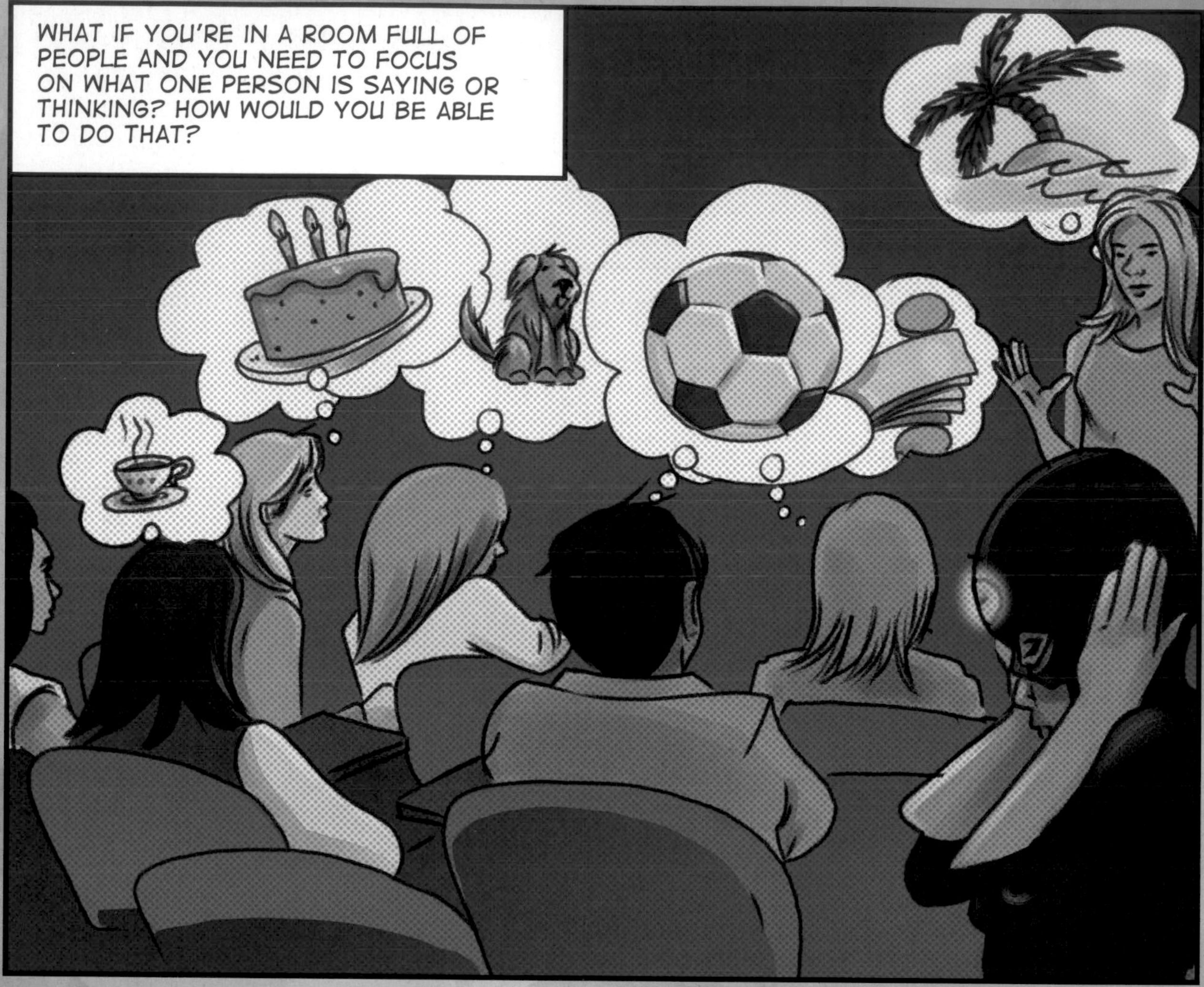
WHAT IF YOU'RE IN A ROOM FULL OF PEOPLE AND YOU NEED TO FOCUS ON WHAT ONE PERSON IS SAYING OR THINKING? HOW WOULD YOU BE ABLE TO DO THAT?

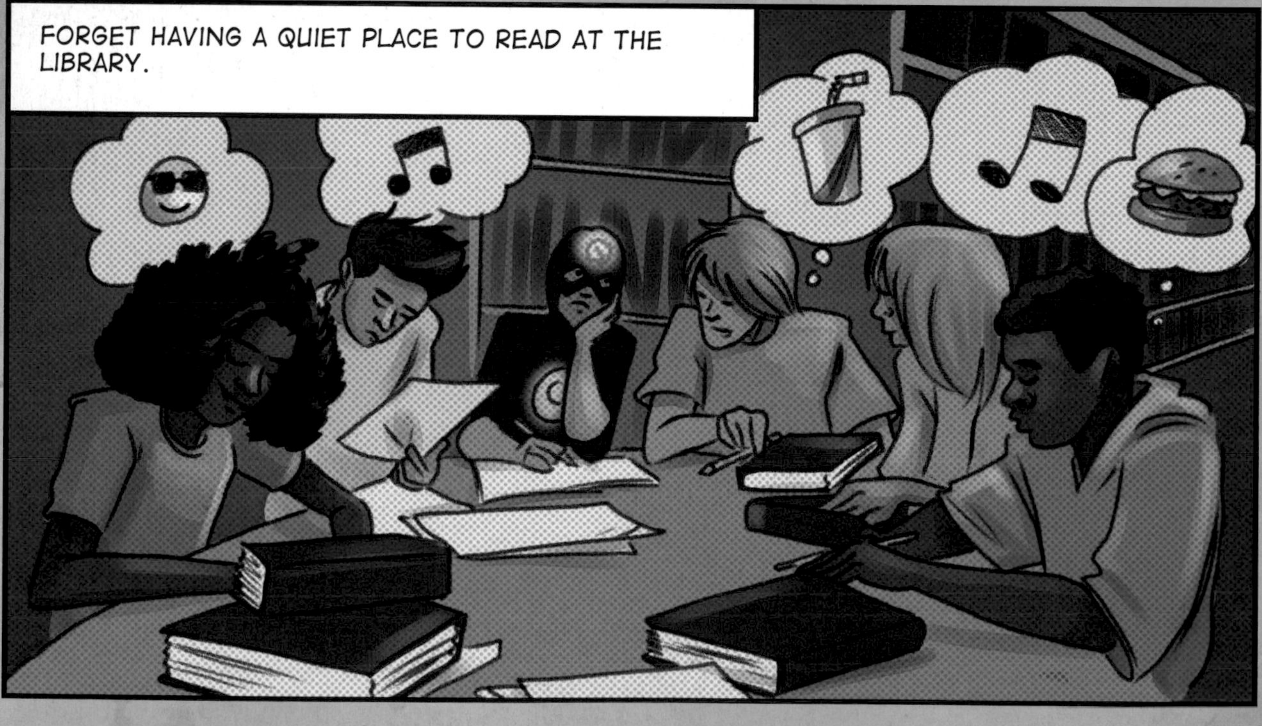
FORGET HAVING A QUIET PLACE TO READ AT THE LIBRARY.

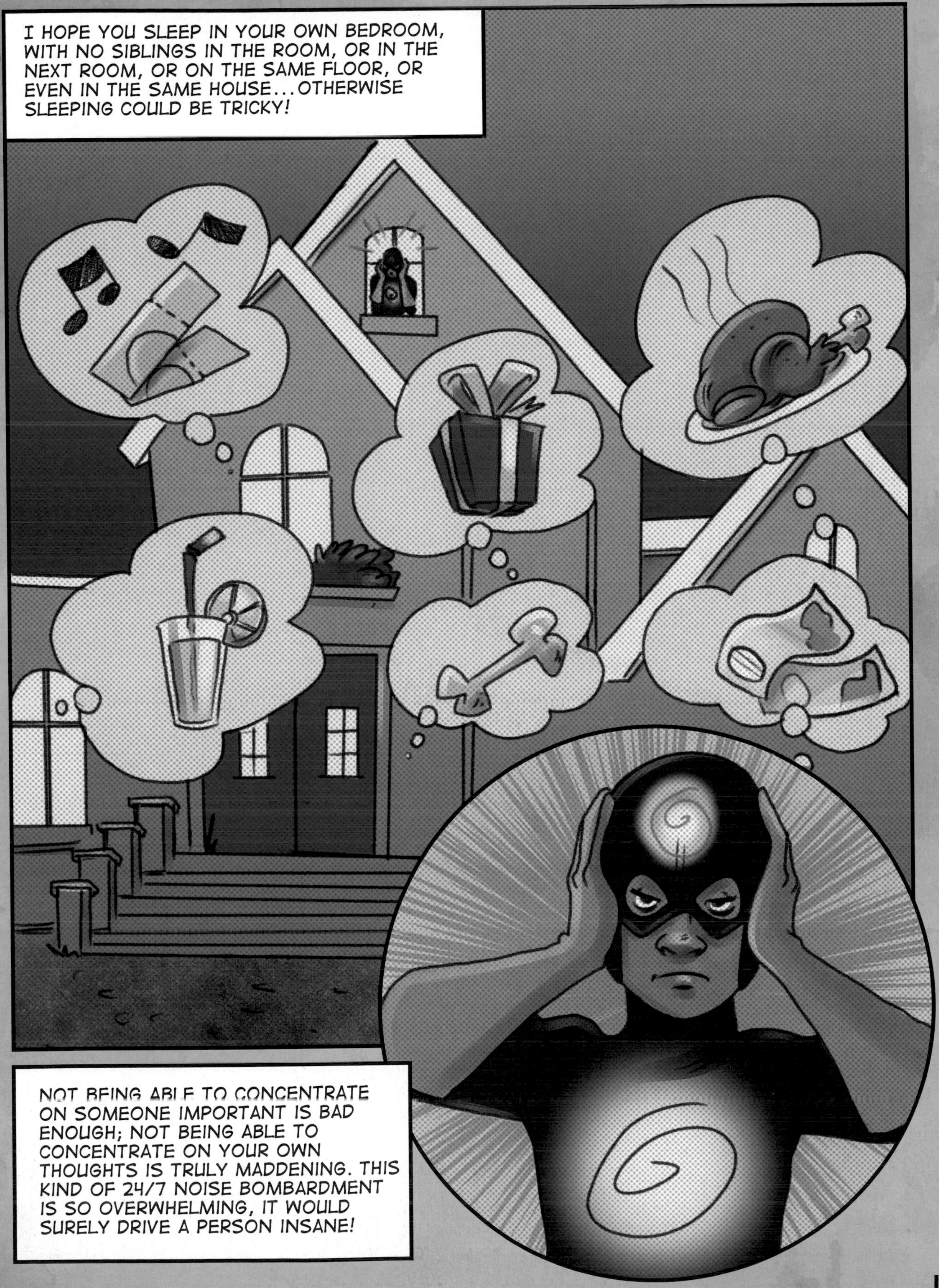
I HOPE YOU SLEEP IN YOUR OWN BEDROOM, WITH NO SIBLINGS IN THE ROOM, OR IN THE NEXT ROOM, OR ON THE SAME FLOOR, OR EVEN IN THE SAME HOUSE...OTHERWISE SLEEPING COULD BE TRICKY!
NOT BEING ABLE TO CONCENTRATE ON SOMEONE IMPORTANT IS BAD ENOUGH; NOT BEING ABLE TO CONCENTRATE ON YOUR OWN THOUGHTS IS TRULY MADDENING. THIS KIND OF 24/7 NOISE BOMBARDMENT IS SO OVERWHELMING, IT WOULD SURELY DRIVE A PERSON INSANE!

ALSO, POLITENESS EXISTS FOR A REASON. IT IS NOT ALWAYS A GOOD THING TO KNOW EVERYBODY'S TRUE OPINION ON EVERYTHING. TELLING A LITTLE LIE CAN PROTECT A LOVED ONE'S FEELINGS AND SOMETIMES WE FILTER WHAT WE SAY IN ORDER TO BE KIND.

DO YOU LIKE MY HAIR?

YES. YOU LOOK BEAUTIFUL.

YOU LOOK LIKE A MAD SCIENTIST BUT I LOVE YOU.

DO YOU NEED HELP?

EUH, QU'EST-CE QU'ELLE A DIT?

AND WHAT IF SOMEONE IS THINKING IN A DIFFERENT LANGUAGE? WOULD YOU UNDERSTAND THEM?

NOW, TRY THINKING ABOUT A PET. IT CAN BE YOURS OR SOMEONE ELSE'S PET. DO YOU HEAR ANY BARKS OR MEOWS? DO YOU REMEMBER TOUCHING THEIR SOFT FUR?

THE ANSWER IS PROBABLY A COMBINATION OF THINGS. THOUGHTS AND MEMORIES ARE NOT ALWAYS FORMED IN COHERENT SENTENCES, OR EVEN IN WORDS.

SOMETIMES IT'S AN IMAGE, SOMETIMES IT'S A SOUND, AND SOMETIMES IT'S A FEELING THAT IS... INDESCRIBABLE.

WE MAY NEVER BE ABLE TO HEAR SOMEONE ELSE'S THOUGHTS. BUT IF YOU PAY CLOSE ATTENTION TO THE PEOPLE YOU TALK TO AND INTERACT WITH, SOON YOU'LL BE ABLE TO PICK UP ON ALL SORTS OF TELL-TALE SIGNS IN THEIR TONE OF VOICE AND BODY LANGUAGE.

RESEARCH HAS SHOWN THAT ONLY 7 PERCENT OF COMMUNICATION IS BASED ON THE ACTUAL WORDS WE SAY. TONE OF VOICE ACCOUNTS FOR 38 PERCENT AND THE REMAINING 55 PERCENT COMES FROM BODY LANGUAGE. MAYBE YOU'VE NOTICED THAT WHEN YOUR FRIEND IS TEASING YOU, HE CAN'T HELP HIS EYEBROW FROM GOING UP SO YOU CAN SEE RIGHT THROUGH WHAT HE'S SAYING. ISN'T THAT A FORM OF MIND READING?

ETERNITY: FOREVER YOUNG!

What if you stayed young your whole life and never grew old?

HAPPY BIRTHDAY! 50 TODAY!

YOUR BODY WOULD NEVER BE AFFECTED BY OLD AGE! NOW, BEAR IN MIND, IMMORTALITY DOES NOT EQUATE TO INVINCIBILITY. YOU WILL STILL FEEL PAIN IF YOU HURT YOURSELF. IT ALSO DOES NOT EQUATE TO SUPER REGENERATION POWERS, WHICH MEANS YOU WOULD HAVE TO GO THROUGH THE NORMAL HEALING PROCESS.

OUCH!

IT JUST MEANS YOU WOULDN'T DIE...EVER! BUT IS THAT REALLY A GOOD THING?

ETERNITY'S SUPERPOWERS
- to stay young forever
- to outlive everyone
- great for accumulating knowledge and skills

HAVE YOU EVER SEEN A SCAR FROM A BAD BURN OR A DEEP CUT? ONCE YOUR TISSUES HAVE BEEN DAMAGED PAST A CERTAIN POINT, IT BECOMES IMPOSSIBLE FOR YOUR BODY TO HEAL ITSELF BACK TO THE WAY IT WAS AND THE SCARS BECOME PERMANENT.

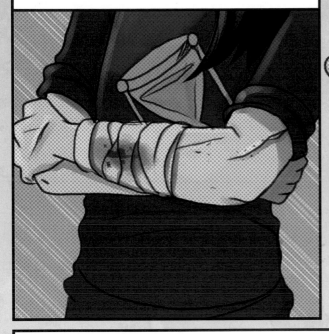

IF YOU LOSE A PIECE OF SKIN ON YOUR FINGERTIP, IT WILL GROW BACK. HOWEVER, IF YOU LOSE AN ENTIRE SEGMENT OF YOUR FINGER, IT WON'T GROW BACK AND YOUR GLOVES WILL NEVER FIT PROPERLY AGAIN.

SCARS ARE THE LEAST OF YOUR WORRIES. IT IS THE ESSENTIAL BODY PARTS THAT DO NOT GROW BACK THAT YOU SHOULD REALLY BE CONCERNED ABOUT, LIKE YOUR EYES, YOUR TEETH, YOUR NOSE, YOUR EARS...

YOU MIGHT THINK THE ODDS OF LOSING A LIMB ARE LOW, AND YOU'D BE RIGHT. BUT EVEN IF IT'S ONLY 0.1 PERCENT PER LIFETIME, IF YOU WERE TO LIVE TEN LIFETIMES, THE ODDS OF YOUR LOSING A LIMB BECOME 1 PERCENT. AFTER 100 LIFETIMES, THE ODDS INCREASE TO 10 PERCENT. AFTER 500 LIFETIMES, IT IS ACTUALLY LESS STATISTICALLY POSSIBLE FOR YOU TO HAVE ALL YOUR LIMBS AND DIGITS ATTACHED. THE MATH OF THIS IS MORE COMPLICATED THAN OUTLINED HERE, BUT YOU GET THE IDEA...

BUT THAT'S NOT ALL. THEN YOU HAVE TO ADD THE ODDS OF LOSING AN EYE OR EAR OR FINGER ON TOP OF LOSING LIMBS...

ANOTHER PROBLEM YOU WOULD HAVE TO FACE IS YOUR MEMORIES. MOST HUMAN BRAINS WORK VERY MUCH LIKE AN OLD DESKTOP COMPUTER. THE MORE MEMORIES IT STORES, THE MORE TIME IT TAKES TO RETRIEVE THE RIGHT INFORMATION.

LET'S IMAGINE THE ACT OF RETRIEVING MEMORIES FROM YOUR BRAIN AS SELECTING A RED APPLE (THE MEMORY) FROM A FRUIT BASKET. IT SHOULD BE A VERY SIMPLE TASK. BUT IF THERE ARE TEN FRUIT BASKETS AND THERE'S ONLY ONE RED APPLE, IT WOULD TAKE YOU A LITTLE LONGER. THE TASK BECOMES EVEN MORE DIFFICULT IF THERE ARE OTHER FRUITS THAT ARE ALSO RED AND ROUND.

HOW MANY SARAHS DO YOU KNOW? HOW MANY DOES YOUR MOM KNOW?

HOW MANY DOES YOUR GRANDMA KNOW? WHAT ABOUT YOUR GREAT-GRANDMA?

IF YOU LIVE UNTIL 100, NAMES AND FACES WILL START TO GET FUZZY FOR YOU. IF YOU LIVE UNTIL 1,000, YOU MIGHT FORGET SOME PEOPLE YOU WERE ONCE IN LOVE WITH. IF YOU LIVE UNTIL 10,000, YOU MIGHT FORGET THE PEOPLE WHO RAISED YOU!

WHAT IF YOU COULD BOOST YOUR MEMORY SO THAT YOU'D REMEMBER EVERY SINGLE THING YOU'VE EVER EXPERIENCED? ISN'T THAT A GREAT IDEA?

WELL, NO. IT IS AN ACTUAL CONDITION CALLED HYPERTHYMESIA. ALONG WITH HAVING THE ABILITY TO RECALL ALMOST EVERYTHING, THE CONDITION ALSO RESULTS IN A NON-STOP, UNCONTROLLABLE STREAM OF MEMORIES OVERFLOODING THE BRAIN, LEADING TO THE PERSON BEING STUCK IN MEMORIES OF THE PAST INSTEAD OF LIVING IN THE PRESENT.

OUR BRAINS FORGET TRIVIAL THINGS FOR A REASON: TO MAKE ROOM FOR MORE IMPORTANT OR RELEVANT THINGS. PATIENTS WITH HYPERTHYMESIA ARE UNABLE TO DO THIS DUE TO ALL THE SPACE BEING CLOGGED UP BY DETAILED MEMORIES OF BORING EVERYDAY TASKS.

AS A RESULT, PEOPLE WITH THIS CONDITION TEND TO NOT DO WELL IN THEIR STUDIES AND CAN BECOME DEPRESSED. IT IS DEFINITELY MORE OF A CURSE THAN A BLESSING.

SOMETHING ELSE TO CONSIDER IS THAT ALL LIVING THINGS ARE CONSTANTLY EVOLVING AND CHANGING, AS THE BRITISH SCIENTIST CHARLES DARWIN (1809-1882) DISCOVERED AND EXPLAINED IN HIS THEORY OF EVOLUTION.

CHARLES DARWIN

LET'S USE BIRDS AS AN EXAMPLE (AS DARWIN DID HIMSELF) TO EXPLAIN THE THEORY. IF ALL THE SEEDS ON AN ISLAND WERE BIG, THEN THE BIRDS WITH BIGGER BEAKS WOULD BE MORE "FIT TO SURVIVE" BECAUSE THEY WOULD BE ABLE TO EAT THE BIG SEEDS.

MORE BIG-BEAKED BIRDS SURVIVING MEANS MORE BIG-BEAK GENES IN THE ISLAND BIRD GENE POOL (THE COLLECTION OF ALL THE GENES BEING PASSED DOWN TO THE NEXT GENERATION OF A SPECIES).

AFTER CENTURIES OF THIS BIG-BEAK ADVANTAGE, EVENTUALLY ALL OF THE SURVIVING BIRDS WOULD HAVE BIG BEAKS ON THIS ISLAND. AND WHEN THESE BIG-BEAKED BIRDS MATE AND HAVE BABY BIRDS...GUESS WHAT?

ALL THE BABY BIRDS WOULD HAVE BIG BEAKS, TOO!

LET'S APPLY THE THEORY OF EVOLUTION TO *HOMO SAPIENS*: HUMANS. AFTER ALL, WE HAVEN'T ALWAYS LOOKED THE SAME WAY AS A SPECIES. WHO KNOWS WHAT HUMAN BEINGS WILL LOOK LIKE 1,000 YEARS FROM NOW? 5,000 YEARS FROM NOW?

MAYBE GIANT EARS WILL BECOME THE NEWEST HOTTEST FASHION TREND, AND EVERYONE WILL EVENTUALLY END UP HAVING GIANT EARS BECAUSE PEOPLE WITH OVERSIZED EARS ARE CONSIDERED ATTRACTIVE AND GET TO PROCREATE MORE, ADDING MORE GIANT-EAR GENES INTO THE OVERALL GENE POOL.

MAYBE THERE WILL BE A FLOOD, GIVING PEOPLE WITH BIG FEET AND WEBBED TOES AN ADVANTAGE BY BEING ABLE TO TREAD WATER BETTER, AND EVENTUALLY EVERYONE WILL END UP HAVING BIG FEET AND WEBBED TOES.

IF YOU LIVE FOREVER, YOU WON'T EVOLVE SINCE EVOLUTION IS A PROCESS THAT HAPPENS THROUGH PASSING DOWN GENES TO THE NEXT GENERATION. YOU WOULD BE STUCK LOOKING THE WAY YOU ARE. NO BIG EARS FOR YOU OR CONVENIENTLY WEBBED FEET IN A FLOODED WORLD...

WE MAY NEVER BE ABLE TO LIVE FOREVER. BUT COMPARE THE AVERAGE WORLD LIFE EXPECTANCY (THE AVERAGE PERIOD THAT A PERSON MAY EXPECT TO LIVE) OF ONLY 29 YEARS OF AGE IN 1770, WITH TODAY. THESE DAYS, THE AVERAGE PERSON IS EXPECTED TO LIVE TO OVER 70 YEARS OLD. THAT'S A HUGE LEAP! DUE TO THE INVENTION OF VARIOUS MEDICINES AND SCIENTIFIC ADVANCEMENTS THAT HELP US FIGHT ILLNESSES, WE ARE NOW LIVING MUCH LONGER. THOUGH WE HAVE FOUND WAYS TO HELP AGING BODY PARTS, WE HAVE YET TO FIND A WAY TO COMPLETELY STOP THEM FROM DECLINING WITH TIME.

THE PERSON TO HAVE LIVED THE LONGEST WAS A FRENCH WOMAN, JEANNE CALMENT (1875-1997), WHO LIVED TO BE 122 YEARS AND 164 DAYS OLD. IMAGINE THAT!

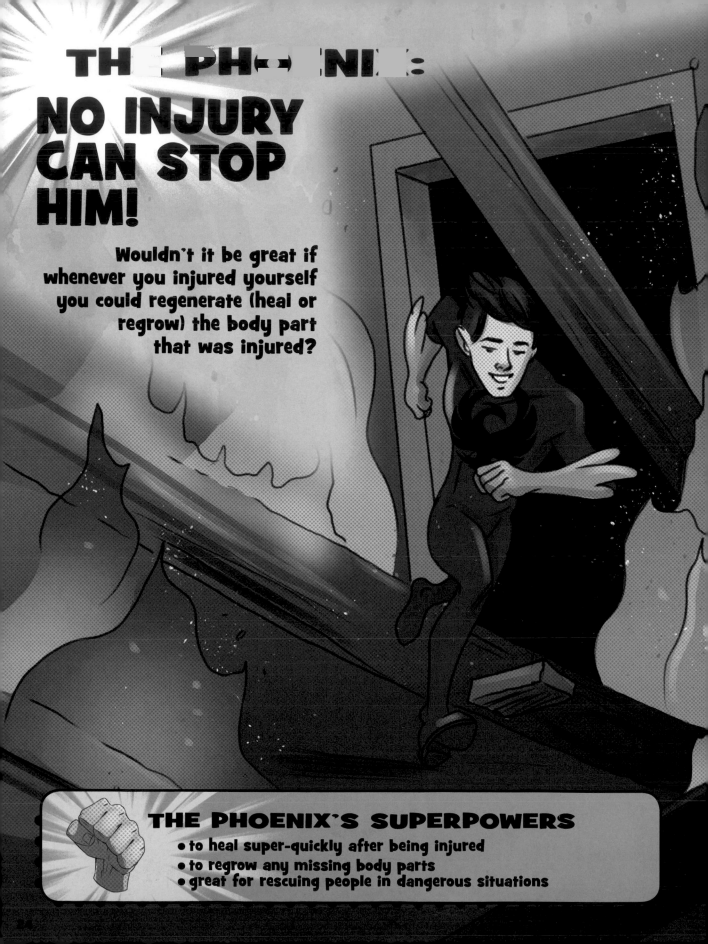

THE PHOENIX: NO INJURY CAN STOP HIM!

Wouldn't it be great if whenever you injured yourself you could regenerate (heal or regrow) the body part that was injured?

THE PHOENIX'S SUPERPOWERS

- to heal super-quickly after being injured
- to regrow any missing body parts
- great for rescuing people in dangerous situations

YOU WOULD BE ABLE TO RESCUE PEOPLE TRAPPED IN BURNING BUILDINGS WITHOUT WORRYING ABOUT BURNS!

OR BE ABLE TO ESCAPE FROM A SHARK-INFESTED POOL WITHOUT WORRYING ABOUT LOSING A LIMB!

BUT, IS IT EVER THAT SIMPLE? BEING ABLE TO REGENERATE WOULD HAVE SOME SURPRISING CONSEQUENCES! AS SOON AS YOU GOT A HAIRCUT, YOUR HAIR WOULD GROW STRAIGHT BACK!

BZZZZ

NOT AGAIN!

AND THIS APPLIES TO NOT ONLY THE HAIR ON THE TOP OF YOUR HEAD, BUT ALSO YOUR EYEBROWS, YOUR EYELASHES, YOUR NOSE HAIR, YOUR EAR HAIR, YOUR ARMPIT HAIR, YOUR CHEST HAIR...

WE DON'T NORMALLY HAVE TO TRIM OUR EYELASHES BECAUSE EVERY TIME ONE BECOMES TOO LONG, IT ALSO BECOMES MORE VULNERABLE AND FALLS OUT. BUT FOR YOU, EVERYTHING WOULD CONTINUE GETTING LONGER AND LONGER BECAUSE EVERY TIME A HAIR FALLS OUT, ANOTHER ONE WOULD GROW BACK TO THE SAME LENGTH IT WAS BEFORE, AND THEN IT WOULD CONTINUE TO GROW!

WHAT ABOUT YOUR BABY TEETH? WOULD THOSE GROW BACK, TOO? IMAGINE HAVING TWO LAYERS OF HUMAN TEETH! LIKE A SHARK, BUT SILLIER!

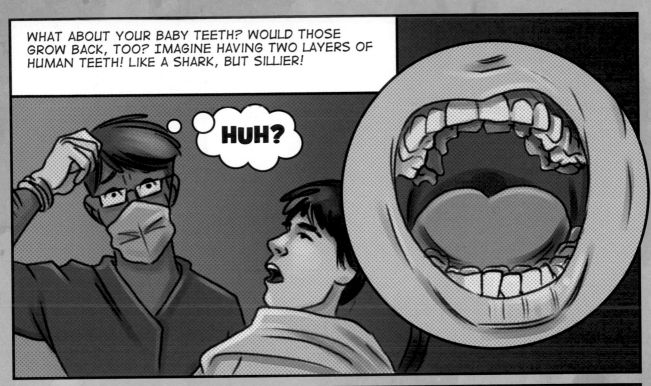

HUH?

THE CALLUSES ON OUR FEET, THE TOUGHENED AREAS THAT ARE THICKER AND HARDER, ARE FORMED AS A RESPONSE TO REPEAT FRICTION. THEY ARE THERE TO PROTECT OUR FEET FROM GETTING HURT AND BLISTERED. BUT IF YOU HAVE REGENERATION, YOUR FEET WOULD NEVER GROW CALLUSES BECAUSE YOUR SKIN WOULD JUST HEAL ITSELF IMMEDIATELY, WHICH WOULD ACTUALLY LEAVE YOUR FEET IN A MORE VULNERABLE STATE.

OUCH!

OR MAYBE THE OPPOSITE WOULD HAPPEN! DID YOU KNOW THAT HUMANS ARE CONSTANTLY SHEDDING SKIN? WE DON'T SHED IT ALL AT ONCE LIKE SNAKES DO, BUT WE SLOWLY SHED OUR ENTIRE OUTER LAYER OF SKIN EVERY 2 TO 4 WEEKS. WE LOSE MILLIONS OF DEAD SKIN CELLS A DAY—ABOUT 30,000 SCALES OF SKIN PER MINUTE! IF YOU KEPT GROWING NEW SKIN CELLS IN ADDITION TO REPLACING THE DEAD SKIN CELLS, HOW THICK WOULD YOUR SKIN END UP BEING?

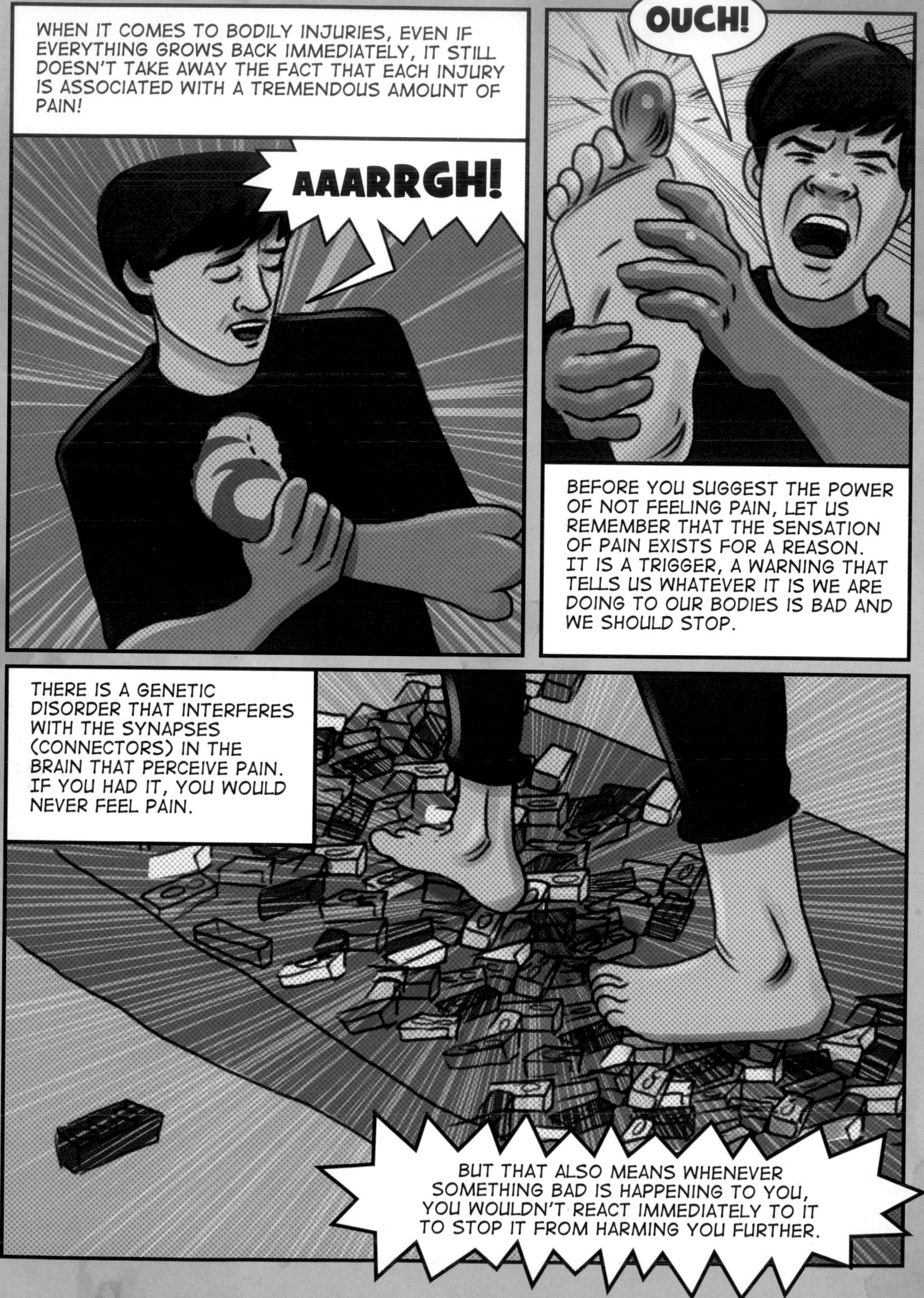

WHEN IT COMES TO BODILY INJURIES, EVEN IF EVERYTHING GROWS BACK IMMEDIATELY, IT STILL DOESN'T TAKE AWAY THE FACT THAT EACH INJURY IS ASSOCIATED WITH A TREMENDOUS AMOUNT OF PAIN!
AAARRGH!
OUCH!
BEFORE YOU SUGGEST THE POWER OF NOT FEELING PAIN, LET US REMEMBER THAT THE SENSATION OF PAIN EXISTS FOR A REASON. IT IS A TRIGGER, A WARNING THAT TELLS US WHATEVER IT IS WE ARE DOING TO OUR BODIES IS BAD AND WE SHOULD STOP.
THERE IS A GENETIC DISORDER THAT INTERFERES WITH THE SYNAPSES (CONNECTORS) IN THE BRAIN THAT PERCEIVE PAIN. IF YOU HAD IT, YOU WOULD NEVER FEEL PAIN.
BUT THAT ALSO MEANS WHENEVER SOMETHING BAD IS HAPPENING TO YOU, YOU WOULDN'T REACT IMMEDIATELY TO IT TO STOP IT FROM HARMING YOU FURTHER.

HEALING AND REGENERATING SOUND MORE MAGICAL THAN PRACTICAL, BUT MEDICAL TEAMS HAVE DONE TREMENDOUS REGENERATION WORK WITH STEM CELL RESEARCH.

STEM CELLS ARE TAKEN FROM EMBRYOS (THE EARLY STAGE IN THE DEVELOPMENT OF A BABY). THESE CELLS HAVE THE POTENTIAL TO GROW AND BECOME ANY TYPE OF CELL IN THE HUMAN BODY.

THEY COULD BE USED TO TREAT SPINAL CORD INJURIES, BRAIN DISEASES SUCH AS ALZHEIMER'S, NERVOUS SYSTEM DISORDERS SUCH AS PARKINSON'S DISEASE, DIABETES, AND EVEN HEART ATTACKS. WE MAY NOT BE ABLE TO REGENERATE WHOLE LIMBS YET, BUT PROSTHETICS ARE GETTING BETTER AND SCIENTISTS ARE EVEN ABLE TO GROW HUMAN EARS ON MICE. NOW, THAT'S SOMETHING!

GLOSSARY

artificial MADE BY HUMAN SKILL AS OPPOSED TO NATURAL

atoms THE BUILDING BLOCKS OF MATTER

bacteria A TYPE OF VERY SMALL ORGANISM THAT LIVES IN AIR, EARTH, WATER, PLANTS, AND ANIMALS, OFTEN ONE THAT CAUSES DISEASE

blister A PAINFUL SWELLING ON THE SKIN THAT CONTAINS LIQUID, CAUSED USUALLY BY CONTINUOUS RUBBING, ESPECIALLY ON YOUR FOOT, OR BY BURNING

coherent BEING LOGICAL AND MAKING SENSE

contract TO MAKE OR BECOME SHORTER OR NARROWER OR GENERALLY SMALLER IN SIZE

element MATTER MADE OF JUST ONE TYPE OF ATOM

friction THE RESISTANCE THAT A SURFACE OR OBJECT ENCOUNTERS WHEN MOVING AGAINST ONE ANOTHER

gene A UNIT OF CODED INSTRUCTIONS THAT LEADS TO A PARTICULAR CHARACTERISTIC, SUCH AS EYE COLOR OR HAIR COLOR, TO BE PASSED ON FROM PARENT TO OFFSPRING

germ A TINY ORGANISM THAT OFTEN CAUSES DISEASES

immune system THE ORGANS, TISSUES, CELLS, AND CELL PRODUCTS, WHICH PROTECT THE BODY BY DETECTING THE PRESENCE OF, AND DISABLING, DISEASE-CAUSING AGENTS IN THE BODY

lymphatic system A NETWORK OF TISSUES AND ORGANS THAT HELP RID THE BODY OF TOXINS (POISONOUS SUBSTANCES), WASTE, AND OTHER UNWANTED MATERIALS. ITS PRIMARY FUNCTION IS TO TRANSPORT LYMPH, A FLUID CONTAINING INFECTION-FIGHTING WHITE BLOOD CELLS, THROUGHOUT THE BODY

matter ANYTHING THAT HAS MASS AND TAKES UP SPACE. IT IS THE STUFF THAT ALL OBJECTS AND MATERIALS AROUND US ARE MADE OF

molecule UNIT OF MATTER MADE OF ATOMS BONDED TOGETHER

muscular RELATING TO MUSCLES THAT CONTRACT TO PRODUCE MOVEMENT

mutation A CHANGE IN A GENE THAT LEADS TO DIFFERENT CHARACTERISTICS, WHICH CAN BE PASSED ON TO THE NEXT GENERATION

neutron A SMALL PARTICLE PRESENT IN THE NUCLEUS (CENTER) OF ALL ATOMS EXCEPT THE HYDROGEN ATOM. NEUTRONS HAVE NO ELECTRICAL CHARGE

nutrient SOMETHING IN FOOD THAT HELPS PEOPLE, ANIMALS, AND PLANTS LIVE AND GROW

organ A PART OF THE BODY OF AN ANIMAL OR PLANT THAT PERFORMS A PARTICULAR JOB. THE HEART, THE LUNGS, THE SKIN, AND THE EYES ARE ALL ORGANS OF AN ANIMAL

periodic table A CHART SHOWING ALL THE ELEMENTS ARRANGED IN A PARTICULAR WAY. THE VERTICAL COLUMNS IN THE PERIODIC TABLE ARE CALLED GROUPS. EACH GROUP CONTAINS ELEMENTS THAT HAVE SIMILAR PROPERTIES

pressure A WAY IN WHICH TO MEASURE HOW MUCH FORCE IS ACTING OVER AN AREA

procreate TO PRODUCE YOUNG

prosthetic A MAN-MADE BODY PART, SUCH AS AN ARM, FOOT, OR TOOTH, THAT REPLACES A MISSING PART

proton A TINY PARTICLE IN THE NUCLEUS (CENTER) OF AN ATOM. A PROTON HAS A POSITIVE ELECTRICAL CHARGE

skeletal RELATING TO THE BONES OF AN ANIMAL, FORMING THE FRAMEWORK OF THE BODY

stretch TO EXTEND OR REACH OUT TO THE FULL LENGTH

telepathy THE ABILITY TO KNOW WHAT IS IN SOMEONE ELSE'S MIND, OR TO COMMUNICATE WITH SOMEONE MENTALLY, WITHOUT USING WORDS OR OTHER PHYSICAL SIGNALS

virus A TINY ORGANISM THAT CAN REPRODUCE ONLY IN LIVING CELLS. VIRUSES CAUSE DISEASE IN HUMANS, ANIMALS, AND PLANTS

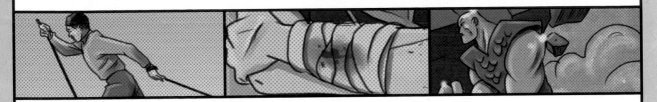

WEBSITES

www.dkfindout.com/uk/human-body/your-amazing-body/
INFORMATION TO IMPROVE YOUR KNOWLEDGE OF HUMAN BODY SYSTEMS AND MORE

www.bbc.com/education/topics/zcyycdm
INFORMATION, VIDEOS, AND QUIZZES ABOUT HOW THE HUMAN BODY WORKS

https://youtu.be/GhHOjC4oxh8
A VIDEO THAT EXPLAINS HOW DARWIN'S THEORY OF EVOLUTION WORKS

https://ed.ted.com/series/?series=superhero-science
AUTHOR JOY LIN'S TED ED VIDEOS ABOUT SCIENCE AND SUPERHEROES

BOOKS

Mind Webs: Human Body BY ANNA CLAYBOURNE (WAYLAND, 2014)

Your Brilliant Body! series BY PAUL MASON (WAYLAND, 2015)

Cause, Effect and Chaos!: In the Human Body
BY PAUL MASON (WAYLAND, 2018)

Anatomy: A Cutaway Look Inside the Human Body
BY HELENE DRUVERT (THAMES & HUDSON, 2017)

INDEX